How To Succeed
In
Any Sales Industry

WRITTEN BY
JASON FITZGERALD

How to Succeed in Any Sales Industry

ISBN: 978-0-9876384-6-5 paperback
ISBN: 978-0-9876384-8-9 eBook

Copyright © Jason Fitzgerald, 2018

First published 2018

All rights reserved. Without limiting the rights under copyright reserved above, no part of this publication may be reproduced, stored in or introduced into a database and retrieval system or transmitted in any form or any means (electronic, mechanical, photocopying, recording or otherwise) without the prior written permission of both the owner of copyright and the above author.

Contents

Chapter 1
Who are you? 1

Chapter 2
What not to forget in sales 6

Chapter 3
Canvassing 10

Chapter 4
Be Prepared 17

Chapter 5
Objections & Rejections 20

Chapter 6
Presentation 23

Chapter 7
Misconception 28

Chapter 8
Research and Development 32

Chapter 9
Honesty 37

Chapter 10
We Sell Ourselves 41

Chapter 11
Rewards 44

Jason Fitzgerald

Chapter 12
Real Estate..47

Chapter 13
Transport & Logistics 53

Chapter 14
Social Media Advertising 56

Chapter 15
Multi-Level Marketing (MLM) 58

Chapter 16
Get out there and sell..............................60

Notes: 62

I am a middle-aged bloke, who has worked in many different roles in my career.

I was always told, "I could sell ice, to an Eskimo," a general cliché, given to someone, who can communicate easily.

Why did I decide to write this book? Well, it's because over time, not only have I seen many things, been educated on many things, but I have been able, to take bits and pieces and make it my own.

What I put in each chapter, is not the key to success, but a guide; to help make you a success. Regardless of what position you hold, or how long you have been in sales or retail.

I have worked in telecommunications, hospitality, transport, cold canvassing, telemarketing & real estate to mention a few. In every position, I have held I've been able, to sell quickly, hold a great close ratio and always kept a customer happy and satisfied with their decision.

Now I have your interest, read on to see how & why.

Kind Regards

Jason Fitzgerald

Chapter 1

Who are you?

You will never see a self-help book or guide to business ethics etc. Tell you that something is wrong, why?

Many businesses set standards, or beliefs, that work for them, or their product, but you and the customers are not them, are you?

Ever been in a store, and you look around and can't see a staff member, to assist you? Or it's the opposite you walk in and before you can even inspect the store or items a staff member is on you.

Why is that? Many reasons come to mind, so let's look at the no staff first. There are often two reasons, firstly lack of staff, for the number of customers.

Secondly staff, who can't be bothered, to approach you, it's just a paycheck, they get known as the laid-back, salespersons.

Now for me, often I analyze the concept of a store, for example; if you go to a Coles supermarket, you don't need a staff member, following you around, to help buy your groceries.

Now if you went into a tire shop, you would like guidance, to make your mind up.

Well, you can either, get too much assistance, or not enough.

When you are the customer, to relate this to an employee; you need to keep that in mind, when you're working.

Often you will see, in a professionally trained store, the staff will great you, with a Smile, ask how you are? Is there anything they can do for you? Or are you looking for something?

Now the laid-back staff may give you a hello, or nothing at all. The greeter may hover, waiting to pounce or guide you, to a sale you may, not even need.

Now, this applies, in any industry, it will not matter, if it's a store, in your home, or when you're walking down the street.

You can easily be bad at sales if you cannot find the balance, this takes the reading, of your customers over time and seeing what works, best for you.

In the chapters, that follow you will gain, more insight into, the wrong salesperson effect.

You always want to impress your boss, over-trying can have the reverse effect also. So, how do you find balance, you need to find your niche first.

Often it can be hard, to do when you first start, with little to no experience. You often have a trainer overseeing, your every move, correcting you on the spot; to what works for them.

This kind of training can also be harmful, many find it overbearing and lose interest quickly.

Many industries, work on a KPI (Key Performance Index) format, this entails meeting set sales figures, that get constructed, based on the amount, of sales, required.

It will also include sales, that may not continue, along with the costs, of business overheads, commissions and so forth.

It will bring on, the greedy, pushy salespersons, because they not only want, to achieve those targets by any means necessary, but to also stand out.

They will want to earn, if commission based, the best amount, or obtain the rewards.

Many of these points, I will, unfortunately, reiterate in the following chapters. It is essential, this is done for you to succeed, in any industry.

Remember there are guidelines, you should never lose focus on, yet so many do; usually due to personal pressures, or lifestyles, you become accustomed too.

You can line, five salespeople up, give them all an apple and a quota. For example, you have 50 apples, to sell, at $1 each and you have, two hours to do so.

Seems easy enough and straight, forward right? Wrong, not everyone can sell, not every person, you see is a buyer and not every location is the same.

So, salesperson 1, leaves the office; with their case of apples. They go sit in a park, at the entrance, as each person, approaches they smile, they say nothing, but have written a sign that says, "apples $1 each".

Let 's say, they sell 20, in two hours not bad, considering they didn't, actively do much, to achieve the sales.

Salesperson 2 goes to a busy intersection, at each light change; they run out to parked cars, smiling, jumping with joy, yelling "Apples for a dollar," they sell 25 in the time allotted.

Salesperson 3 takes their box, to a train station, as passengers come and go through the gate, this salesperson greets them, with a smile and politely says "Hi, how are you? I have apples for a $1, would you like to buy one", they sell 35 apples.

Salesperson 4 takes their box, to an office building, obtains permission, from reception to go around and ask, "if anyone would like, to buy some apples, at $1 ea." and sells 40.

Salesperson 5 takes their apples, to a juice stand, they offer them, the whole box for $50. They sell them, all in one transaction, done and dusted

Which sales person is the laziest? Which one is the most professional? Who is most aggressive?

Now you're thinking, well Number 1, is the laziest, Number 4 is the most professional and number 2, is most aggressive; jumping out in moving traffic.

If you picked those numbers, you're not wrong, you're just not looking, at all the facts. You may see just numbers; maybe you have different answers, to what I believe, that's not wrong; it means you evaluate differently, to a situation than others.

Now, I believe number 5, is the laziest. Why do you ask? It's simple, they only approached, one place, got the sale, done nothing for rest of the time.

Number 3 is the most, professional they took the time, to approach people, politely ask, "how they were?" then offer something to buy.

Number 4 is most aggressive, they know disturbing a business, to sell their items, is a disruption. Does salesperson four care no! They want the sales.

We will go into this more in different chapters.

Chapter 2

What not to forget in sales

It may seem, that I wonder when typing all this out. That is, because my brain wanders, with so many examples and facts.

Trying to put, all that into words, to make sense, to some else is not always an easy task.

In this chapter, I will talk about things; I stick to in Sales, no matter the industry.

Now, when you generally undertake, a sales position, you may or may not be familiar with the industry. You may or may not know the product or the competition.

It is important, to know all these, sales is an interpretation industry, you must perceive the buyer, the market or the result.

When in training, your employer, is trying to fabricate, you into a version or extension of them. They want you to perform, in a nearly robotic format, to achieve results.

They often, repeat over and over spiels, sayings, scenarios, objections, reasons why. Their famous saying is, "We have tried, many concepts and found this, to be the most effective, if you practice this, it will become second nature."

Sorry to say this, but it's not, completely true. Adapting is the most, effective way to be trained. Yes, you must be fluent, in whatever your selling, but to speak like someone else, is never easy.

Why is that? Because, we are individuals, as individuals, we need to become, fluent in us to sell.

I have always, said some simple rules, and these are; Never be anyone but you. Never sell anything, you wouldn't buy.

Never sell anything, you know, is dishonest or false. Always dress to the target audience, and always be honest & respectful always. Lastly always back your product.

One thing, I have heard often, from customers; is that a salesperson, made them feel stupid, pressured, or like they were wasting, that salespersons time.

Often it happens from targets known as KPI's or quotas. When staff gets driven, to be result focused; otherwise they don't have a job.

The funny thing is, you won't have a job if customers, do not buy in the first place, that results in a closed business anyway.

I always have, had a saying "100 customers at a $1, is better than one customer for $100". Now if you don't understand this, saying you are in the wrong business or job.

Long before today's social media, as a major influence, salespersons relied on word of mouth, now this works for you and against you.

Now if you upset, 1 or 100 people, they, in turn, tell of their experience. It has an enormous effect, on your business.

Now if you impress, 100 people instead of 1, this has an enormous, benefit to the business. For you and your business to be successful, you need repeat customers.

Now if one person, tells one person, you now have two customers. If 100 customers, tell 100 people, you now have 200 customers.

Businesses often, forget this fact, with the Progression, of social media influencers, the average person, or a business, can be either made or ruined quickly.

I see so much now, with social media, how quick people are to criticize, or recommend; I am even one of those persons.

Why would I support, a business I had a bad interaction with when I can recommend a business or person, I have had a great interaction.

Before social media, you would hear from friends, about certain experiences, good or bad. You would ask, from a friend or relative, if they knew of a place, to obtain a product or service.

Now with social media, it takes just two seconds, to post or ask the same thing. Now anyone in that region or page can share, the good and bad for all to see; this can have a snowball effect.

If your business, does not get the support, it's very hard to break through, the negativity these days.

So, you need to set yourself apart, from the stigma, and the aging world, of social media. Make it work for you.

How do you do this? It is very simple, follow the rules and beliefs, I stated earlier, in this chapter of what, I always make sure I do.

In the following chapters, we will look at industries, the good the bad, how to make sure you do well and succeed.

Chapter 3

Canvassing

This is one of the oldest industries, now one of, the most hated. Why has it become so hated?

Mainly because of the way, things got done in the eighties & nineties.

It was the system, before social media, in which a business, could achieve a higher rate of sales. It was designed to bring a product or service to you.

Usually, it is something, you may or may not need. Something you did not realize, you need or even started to work out, where to go to get it.

When I first got into this industry, back in the early 90's, we would target businesses, in a certain area, as we sold advertising, for booklets for certain organizations.

The training was simple: we were handed a spiel, a Phone did a couple of rehearsed calls, with other staff.

Then we were sat, at a desk given a call sheet, and told to go for it.

Now telemarketing, door to door, are all cold leads. You are bringing, something to someone, who had not contacted you first. Now, if you were good at talking, you did well.

The issue with phones, is people do not see, the person contacting them, they can easily hang up. Door to door, can be more confronting, as it is face to face, you never know, whose door, it is your knocking on.

There are simple ways, to do these types of jobs. Unfortunately, so many people, over the years, badgered people, that it also becomes a pest industry.

I was very successful, at them both, back then the door to door, was great exercise. Depending on what you, had to sell, not only do you meet all types, but you can read a person's demeanor, this helps with the sale.

To be successful, at telemarketing, you must learn, to hear; the persons demeanor.

Now in general, the owner or sales manager, have written a spiel, which was a robot response, dictation; that you got trained, to do like a robot.

You got taught, to not waste time, on dead calls, just ring next number go again. It's a number game, the more numbers, you crunch; the more sales you get.

Now unless taking payment, then and there, you could also lose sales. Laws state; with cold calls as you contacted them, they are entitled to a 10-day cooling off period, in which they can change their minds and cancel the sale.

Now a ruthless salesperson had lots of cancelations, but a great salesperson never had many cancels. Back in Chapter 2, I spoke about things, to be a successful salesperson. Here is another point; to lessen the cancelations, build rapport, with the customer, but how do you do this with robotic spiels?

It's easy, you modify, the spiel to you. You are the reason; most people buy in the first place.

I have found, if I, keep a spiel, stating the information required, I could tailor, the conversation to flow.

It is less of a hassle, if the whole conversation, is normal, compared to robotic.

How can you change it, when the boss, was always stating; do not diverge from this it works!

You make sure you utilize, the spiel in and around, your rapport building.

Below, is an example, of a spiel. Then I changed it, with the rapport, which is different for everyone.

Spiel Common

Phone rings

Cust: "Hello."

You: "Hi, this is Jason, Is Mr. Thatcher Available?

Cust: "Speaking, what can I do for you?"

You: "Well, I am calling you today, to tell you; about this fantastic opportunity, and how you can, become involved."

Cust: "Sorry, I don't have time, I have work to do."

You: "Well I do understand Sir, but this will take, about 5 minutes of your time, you wouldn't want; to be left out of a community project, now would you?"

Chapter 3   Canvassing

"Your customers, are how your business thrives, I am sure; you spend valuable time and money finding, ways to bring customers to your store?"

Cust: "Look I said I am not interested, I don't have time to deal, with telemarketers, I am very busy!"

Ok, I could go on and on, as often these spiels do. You catch the drift, I hope. Now let's do it, with introducing your style and see the difference.

Spiel Tweaked

Phone rings

Cust: "Hello.

You: "Hi, this is Jason, Is Mr. Thatcher, Available?"

Cust: "Speaking, what can I do for you?"

You: "Mr. Thatcher I hope all is well with you; I am calling you today, to tell you about this fantastic opportunity, for your community, also how you can, become involved - Now I understand, you are a very busy person, if you are unavailable, to talk with me now, is there more suitable time; we can chat for 5-10 mins?"

Cust: "Sorry, I don't have time, I have work to do."

You: "Fully understand Sir, but this will take about, 5 minutes of your time. I am happy to contact you, at a more appropriate time for you, even when you get done, for the day and sitting down to a cold drink, can also call back later in the week; whichever suits you."

Cust: "I suppose, I can spare 5 minutes now, so get to the point."

You: "I appreciate you giving, me the time Mr. Thatcher - We are doing a community booklet, that will be distributed, to local organizations, in your area - it contains vital information, for the youth regarding drugs, crime, etc. I am sure you understand: the importance of information, like this for our youth; now the great thing today, is we are offering local business, the opportunity, to help us produce, the booklet, by your advertising in it, your payment helps us, cover the cost of printing and distribution."

Cust: "Well yes, more is needed, most days I have young kids, hanging around our business, causing grief: more education needs to be done."

So, as you can see these spiels, can be written multiple ways, they have so many scenarios, they can contain, direct ways, to indirectly, get yes and no answers, all through them.

The difference is how you approach, from you in the first place. The way your voice sounds, can play a key down the line, to the questions you ask.

Yes, we all want to crunch numbers, achieve targets, what is the point of making, 100 calls selling to 20, then 15 cancels, your left with five sales.

Wouldn't you rather; make 50 calls, sell 20, with zero cancelled, have 20 confirmed sales.

How is this possible; easy spend time, don't rush the client, build rapport? Ask questions, about the person, their life, record the answers, on a piece of paper.

Be sure to mention names, interests, throughout the conversation; this shows you are paying attention, to them. People, love to talk about them, they will always remember, the person who remembers, what they said.

Obviously, with doing door to door you can't write down responses, don't be in a rush to knock on 100 doors. When I used to knock on doors, after saying my name and why I was there, the next thing was a compliment, about their garden or home, even their outfit.

It loosens the tension, of a stranger knocking, on their door. They appreciate, when you notice something, they take pride in, that they enjoy like bikes, cars, even pets.

The more progressive way, of cold canvassing now, is social media ads. By providing a quick video/picture, of a product you may catch, a buyer's interest, they then can interact, to gain more information.

One more form is TV sales channels when they first started; this is effectively taking out, the coldness side, also the direct approach, because now your enticing them, to ring and buy on impulse.

It gets you inside, every home without rejection, they simply ring, buy, instead of being the seller, you become, the sales support.

The biggest way, to be successful, in these kinds of jobs, is not to be deflated, by knockbacks and the word no.

Once said to me, "Every no, is closer to a yes." But again, don't sell something, this way if you don't believe in it, trust it, back it, can be honest about it.

Do you ever notice; when a telemarketer rings you, you ask them, "what is the company name and a contact phone number?" yet they pretend, not to hear you.

They may try to avoid, speak fast or simply hang-up, that's because; they have something to hide, they just want the sale, yes, the pushy salesperson?

I always gave details, phone numbers, and the reason will surprise you why. I knew, if that person, had enjoyed talking to me, once the product arrived, was all it was, as well as, what I explained.

They will tell their friends. Guess what; they would hand out my number. Not only did this also increase my sales but gave me access to more buyers' and referrals all the time.

Chapter 4

Be Prepared

Sounds easy enough right? Wrong, many times people, only take the time, to know the basics.

Enough to sell a product, they don't research, to see if there is competition, or similar products, these days with bad or good reviews.

Of course, this does not relate, to every product I remember, when I did a barpersons course, now I had experienced, many varieties of alcohol. I knew how they tasted, but when doing the course, they told us, "to not drive to the course."

I thought well that's fair; we are sampling alcohol, they have a moral obligation, to our safety.

Now not everyone, in the course, wanted to try different wines, beers, spirits. The teacher stated clearly. It's not about your personal choice; it's about your customers.

They are right, a bartender is not a servant, to just supply, what you order. They are also the salesperson, for the establishment. Part of their job is to educate or entice you, to try other products, of course, generates more in the till.

Now imagine, you go to a bar, you always drink xxxx beer, but this bar is not a stockist of that product.

Because they have never, sold volumes in the past, so you ask; what another beer, might be good to try. Now if that barperson, has never tried it how are they going to sell it?

It may not be their choice of drink, but they have a duty, to explain and sell to the consumer.

Same with any industry, except supermarkets. Imagine going to a supermarket; you have never tried tuna in a can. You asked, an employee, to tell you the difference; they cannot get most times unless they are a devoted tuna eater.

But in the years gone by, another trade, that is going wayside, to big business was the fruiter. They knew all about the produce.

When I was 15, I worked for a fruit shop; they taught me heaps. I tried things, my parents never bought, that way when a customer asked, I could explain about the product.

When I was 16, I worked for Coles, in the fruit and veg section and my knowledge, was often put to good use, but you don't see it much anymore, in these big chains.

I have sold advertising, Kirby vacuums, Gutter protection, roof restorations, all from cold canvassing. I did my research, I tried & tested the products.

I drilled my employers, about every facet, of the product, to see how much; they backed it, as well as knew about it, all before I would sell it.

Chapter 4 Be Prepared

I had to believe and trust the product first. I needed, to know I can run, into a customer one day, and they would say hello or thanks. Not you're the bastard, who sold me that crap.

I learned very early, on in my work life, that often people buy, the seller, not always the product. It is true, I have asked people; "why you bought that?" and they said, "I liked the salesperson that simple."

When asked, if they liked the product? Some would say, they never used it, or it was not, what we had explained to us.

I believed in every product, or service I sold. I was always, backing the products up, by making sure customers, knew they could ring if they had any further questions.

Look, you can do a full one-hour demonstration, on how to use a Kirby Vacuum, by the time theirs arrive, they have forgotten 50%, of its uses or how to use it.

The customer is never completely satisfied, until, they see the finished product, or experienced the entire product themselves.

Education is a sales tool, the more you educate, a buyer the more confident they become. Buyers most times, will not even realize, they are pre-selling, an item for you, in the way they talk their friends.

Make sure, you always follow up, after a sale, this is not only, an opportunity for referrals, but a great way, for customer feedback on the product. You can take back, that feedback, to your boss.

You can also, tell it to another customer. The more, you have in your, basket of tricks, the better you become at sales.

Chapter 5

Objections & Rejections

Objections are just one facet, of sales, but it's also the reason, you may or may not succeed. Every buyer is skeptical. Have a look at yourself; when you buy, do you question, the service or product?

Of course, we do, as sales professionals, we also too often can see the bullshit. Unless the other salesperson, is so finely tuned, they swindle you up.

So, why do we often, get so many rejections, or objections? Simple there is an underlying issue, the customer has. It can be finances, doubt, unsuited, or they want to make you, earn the sale.

If you get trained well, you will have been taught, to handle knockbacks, the business has encountered. There are ways of getting around them. Some trainers will tell you, the more questions, you ask, the sooner you learn the answers.

It can also, help you see, sooner if you're wasting your time, or if you must work harder.

Leading questions help access what to do, for example. Mr. Fletcher, can you see; how this product, will save you time? If they answer, "No," then you have not explained, the time saving of the product.

So, they lack, information to decide. If they answer "yes," you can then follow with, "so, Mr. Fletcher, if your happy with the time, it saves you, then you being, the intelligent man, you are, you can see, it will allow you more time, to do what you like, as you said, earlier fishing."

The more questions, you ask the more, it directs you how to handle, such objections and to lead to a sale.

You will always, have that one buyer, that believes in the product. They can see its benefits and are kicking, themselves to buy it.

Financially they may, not be in a position, right now. A pushy salesperson can ruin a sale completely, by continuing the sale.

Sometimes, it is easier to say, "Mr. Fletcher, I have shown you, all I can, I have explained everything, to you; I can see you really want it, How about, I leave you my details, when things change, give me a call - please feel free to pass, on my details, to any friends, you can see would benefit."

Of course, many companies, after the finance, being the main issue, incorporated payment options over the years. Often leads to two things, one good and one bad.

First, the wrong thing, is you have placed the person, into another bill, they may not be able to afford. The second, it may have been, the only way, the person, could buy it, then or ever.

The way you, word the sentence, or question can provoke, an objection, or close a sale. Wording things differently, sometimes tricks the brain, into a different response.

It can also trigger, anger or frustration. The Buyer may think you're an idiot because you're not listening, or you are too pushy.

The way you say, a sentence or ask a question, even the sound of your voice triggers different responses too.

If you sound frustrated, or to firm, they can back off. If you sound, too friendly, then they will think that you are begging.

Sales is not a black and white game, it is multi-colored, it comes in all shade's, directions, applications, the technique is what creates, great salespeople.

Always put yourself, in the customer's shoes, what if you had a bad day, went to the store, didn't want to talk, to someone and you get what sounds, like the nagging salesperson.

Next, you're in the firing line, for a pile of objections, because they want, you to feel bad too.

Remember, in the chapter about spiels, if you become robotic, in your presentation, then you often, focus just on the sale, you are now gathering the objections because you portray, that's what you want.

Reading peoples responses, body language, answers, can and should change your delivery. Inadvertently it changes the process of the sale; it can eliminate, objections and rejections.

Chapter 6

Presentation

Now you would be thinking, this chapter is on how to present your sales pitch, well its half, the other half, of a presentation is you.

Now, there are many salespersons, that will tell you how you present will help you sell. To a point, this is correct.

I mean, in the old days, how someone presented themselves, it was believed, they were of good ethics. They were a person, to be trusted, but as the years, went on, most also said, it was a way to hide, the true person, behind the appearance.

Of course, we have all, seen the well-dressed salesperson, in a flash car, in the industry. Will this mean, they are good, at their job? Are they just lucky, or can portray themselves well?

I used to believe; if you wanted to succeed, in sales, you had to look the part, sound the part, be the part so that people will believe.

Lucky for me, this didn't last long, as I grew with experience, I followed the changes, over the years. I watched buyers, look for something more than clothes and cars.

They wanted a genuine, down to earth, honest salesperson.

Look at this way, you can walk into, a fast food restaurant, as they are in retail sales. They are all dressed, to present themselves, along with the company.

You do not see, them in suits, to serve you, unless, it is the owner or manager, even these days, they don't dress, too much different to the staff.

But you still buy the food, unless of course, you walked in, they were all wearing singlets, stunk, looked unhygienically unsafe, also the place, was so filthy, you may think twice, about ordering, right?

You know, I am most comfortable, in a pair of thongs, also known as flip-flops, in other places: a pair of ratty shorts, shirt or singlet. I also look after my appearance.

Now some would be thinking, I am a bogan, is that a bad thing?

Well, I can tell you, it's not. If I present myself respectively, speak with surety and honesty, educate you, on a product, also back what I say. Why? should it, matter what I wear?

If I was wearing, a suit, in a car parts store, you came in, covered in grease, is it a match? Should I judge you, think; oh, here we go, this bloke is dirty, he can't afford shit.

Now of course, if you present, the information, regarding products or services, people will make, an informed decision to buy.

Every industry has a different way, to showcase themselves. Being a good salesperson, unless you only work, in one environment, is to adapt. Just like an actor, they must change, to every script, too don't they?

Every salesperson will have a different way, to portray, any presentation, based on what works, for them.

Sometimes, things work for you, other times, you need to change, to suit your style.

Have you often noticed, that even an experienced salesperson, will see a newer salesperson, in action, hear, or see their presentation?

It will give them, another avenue, to utilize when they sell. Many experienced salespersons want you to learn, from their experience. It often saves you time, getting that sale, but it also can eliminate many objections.

Present, for the person and the occasion. Learn to communicate, on that person's level. If you are dealing with a laid-back person, no point is coming in, gung-ho like you, are presenting to a corporation.

I have been able, to watch and observe, the actions, along with the deliveries of some great salespersons. From this, I have always taken bits, turned it into my way, it's called adaption.

I am also adaptable, to the industry. I can easily slot into, any sales section and deliver, no matter what the product is, or the style of the business.

So, I can dress down or up to suit. I can change how I speak or present, I can also modify myself, to seem inexperienced, to learn, until I master my technique, for that job.

Customers have an idea, of the salesperson, based on the way, they present or speak and act. They also have a perception, about the industry, along with, what they expect, from that industry.

Every job in some format has a sales avenue

Let's look at a Pastor; now you're thinking, what sales, has a church got to do. Well, a church sells itself, to the followers, to have them interact, as well as, help the church.

They need to, keep member numbers up. Now the priest, sells himself, to the followers, if you have a difficult priest, he may offend followers, this causes them not to attend.

Now, I have been married three times. Most recently, in 2018. Previously I used, a celebrant, even though, I was raised in a religious family, as an adult, I no longer followed. My partners were not followers, of a religion.

For my 3rd marriage, we decided, to use a priest from my religion. Now members, of my family, had raved, about how this priest, was such a nice guy (see referral of sale).

So, we made, an appointment, went in discussing our marriage ceremony.

Now usually, a priest will want, to use the church, also include certain religious sections. We stated, exactly, how we, wanted our wedding.

Chapter 6 Presentation

We wanted it brief, we cut most, of the crap out, so it was, quick and simple. We also wanted, to be married by the water.

Now, when we first, met the Priest, he showed up wearing shorts, shirt and sandals this was great. It relaxed me. When I grew up, my priest always, wore dress pants and shirts, as this was the image portrayed.

These days, my most comfortable, clothing are shorts singlet and thongs (flip-flops or jandals).

Now, we explained, our wedding attire, were men in suit printed t-shirts, shorts and thongs. The bride wore a dress, it was not, an elegant wedding dress, but was something, she was comfortable.

We had also instructed, the small gathering to wear comfy clothing.

Our priest loved our concept; to him, it was about love and simplicity, not dollars. It was laid back, no stress and no mortgage.

Now, for the wedding, the priest wore his traditional attire. He delivered, a short, but effective ceremony, that took, a whole 7-8 mins, we were then married.

Now, this priest, tells his congregation, of how he loved, our wedding and format. Those that attended, our wedding, still comment today, about how our priest was so lovely and laid back.

Now, this is what a presentation is about, it's not about, how manipulative, you can get for a quick sale.

You also need, to make buyers feel at home, this in return, will get you, referrals and recommendations.

99% of customers, do not buy the product, although they do, often they buy you too!

Chapter 7

Misconception

Now as salespersons, we must be quick, to evaluate buyers. We may feel, at times, that we can tell them, apart quickly. Sometimes, we get it wrong; I have often been informed, I am too, customer focused.

Now, am I too focused; or am I, a smart salesperson? In previous chapters, I have explained, that buyers are the reason, for your growth. They will tell, people about you, the business, the products, also it can be, the opposite too, in a negative way.

So, many times I have heard, an experienced salesperson say, "don't waste time, on time wasters," you can learn, who is just leading you on easily.

There are many types, of buyers, the here and now, the well informed, the learners, they don't care they just want it, as well as the not in a hurry, as it must be just right when we buy.

So, the here and now buyers, are those who need something, walk in, go right to what they want, then buy. Products like groceries, car parts, food, phones, etc. The well informed, are those who, do research, they want to know, all they can about everything, they wish to buy.

Therefore, as I said earlier, know your product and its competitors, if a buyer feels you, don't know, they will go elsewhere.

The time wasters, usually do not, ever plan on buying, they may or may not, have the money, or are still deciding. They may think, they are caught in a fad, do they need it; or want the product or service.

It also covers, the not in a hurry to buy, as well. The difference is the ones that were not in a hurry it means they do want it but are wanting, to see if prices change, or a newer version is coming.

Of course, the number one buyer, the skeptic, there is an issue, or fault in everything, before they part with cash, they want to make sure, they have drilled you completely.

Now the aggressive salesperson, who wants a sale, no matter what. They chase multiple sales, or are out, smash expectation.

They do this, too make sure they earn well. Often will move quickly, in an order amongst buyers to find the sale.

Of course, we all want to earn, achieve the expectations, what happens to the buyers, they leave behind? I mean someone must deal with them.

We come back to referrals, because, the ones who bought fast, may or may not, promote you, the product, in a good way. The ones left over will do the same.

The customer, does not see that you, are busy, driven by KPI's, they see, how you treat and deal with them, sometimes others, but mainly them only.

How do we find balance? Well, I treat them, all the same. Why be categorizing them?

When I worked, in real estate, some salespersons, where all about how soon, they could sell the house, get their commission, to please the homeowners.

I fed off, their scraps, to start with and guess what? Those they forgot bought, from me and my service.

Now, will go into more specific details, in other chapters, as to why, but right now, it's about understanding the buyers. These are the people that keep you employed.

The old slogan is that the customer is always right. Some cases, this is true, because if a customer, goes away and says you or your business, are shit, to enough people, they know you will close doors, so then, they are right.

If a customer, is not happy, because they want assistance, now it's not always a refund, maybe it's more guidance, a better deal.

You need to evaluate, and listen to the buyer, to make them happy again; therefore they are always right.

The best and worst critic, of a business, is the customer. No matter how wrong, they may be, at times it's that dealing, or feeling, that goes on forever.

The more dealings, you have with the consumer, the more prepared, you are for each buyer to sell too. You will adapt and foresee, by the interaction, what may become an issue, a grumpy customer or a happy customer.

Reading customers, is a hard thing, to teach you. You either can or can't, do it. Yes, we can all get it wrong, at times.

By ensuring, you develop a simple, yet effective method, to be the best at your position, can change the whole, interaction with a customer.

Never, give a customer, something you can't back, don't promise the world, when it's not yours to give.

Be the customer, when selling, if you can't sell, to yourself, how can you; sell to others.

Chapter 8

Research and Development

By now, I think we have, a good understanding, with the difference between sellers and buyers. Everything that is in my head it is hard to write, on paper. Every time, you put words on paper, like when talking, each scenario can lead to more information.

So, what defines research and development? Well, it's about learning and implementing, that knowledge, into your business or job.

Everything, in this world, has a purpose or was created by a person, who saw something, that they needed or thought others would need, or could benefit.

Houses were invented, as a more comfortable form of living. Vehicles were invented, to enable further travel, or to carry loads. Food became packaged, to make it more accessible, or too last longer, instead of hunting and foraging, so often.

Some common mistakes, people make is they design things, to their taste. Everyone's tastes are different, as are their needs, so this leads us, to research and development.

I often, can walk into a business, drive past one and see what its faults may be. Cafes are big business, these days. Everyone sees one somewhere, or owners create one based on their tastes.

Location is a vital point, to the success, of a business, as areas grow, so will access to businesses.

We often see suburbs miles, from some shopping districts. You may see, a small convenience shop, built to cater to basic and emergency needs.

Before, placing a business, in a location, do the research. You must, look at who is your market, and what kind of restrictions, to your business in that area. Things like operating times, accessibility, frontage size and parking.

There are many, brands of coffee. How do you decide; what is going to work, before you open.

Well, you need to find suppliers, of these products, test them, what may taste good, to you, may not please, the customer.

When researching pricing, there is no point having a premium coffee blend, that puts your costs, out of the market. If people cannot afford to buy it, no point being too cheap either if it tastes no good, customers won't be back.

Explore the surrounding competitors, with the ease of Google research; can be often acquired, a lot quicker, these days too.

Search demographics look at feedback, especially items, you may or may not want, to include. Remember the business, is not about your wants, it's about the customers, wants and needs.

Products need research, say you work in an electronics store. There are other brands and products, all differing costs or inclusions.

When a customer, comes to you, they want your guidance, to buy what is right for them.

I will and for this, let's use a laptop. I will google brands, models, pricing, also look at the feedback. Everything you read on the internet is not true, but the more, you read and search, the more information, will make up your knowledge.

I then monitor store catalogs either online or via their webpage. I can see, what it is selling for, this educates me, to know when the right time is to buy.

It won't always happen, this way sometimes, you need something now, buy it then two weeks later it's on sale, and you're like 'grrrr'.

If only, I had waited to buy, you cannot know when that will happen; we are not psychic.

A salesperson, will not want, to be uniform like everyone else while serving a customer, what if that customer, has done research. You cannot help them, achieve a purchase, if you know less than them, they will go to someone, who can.

Of course, some customers, do enough research they waltz in, go straight to the laptop, they want and checkout. Some may be, seeking information, from you, to help them, make sure, they are making the right decision, before parting with their cash.

Other research, for example; maybe more complex. When I worked in transport & logistics, I had to know, who my competitors were, their pricing, their service, how they implemented it, how they made sure it delivered and on time, every time.

No point going, to the customer and saying, "hey I can do your products, for $1, I can pick them up at 4 pm daily, also guarantee, that they, will be delivered the next day if the business

Charges $2 and can only pick up weekly, but deliveries are every 3-5 days.

Research and development are how you, promise or guarantee a service. For that product or service, you better be damn sure, you do you make it happen.

I had a customer once, I delivered to at 3 am, every morning. He was in the earth moving business, often he needed parts, for his machines.

Now, when I got this customer, I networked with other drivers, in different areas, to make sure, if this customer, ever needed something urgently, they could get it, on the line haul truck to me.

Now, often I changed my runs, to suit my customers. I would go to the depot, at midnight, sort my freight, that had arrived from linehaul.

My run was timed, based on a specific order. Calculated on the speed of my loading and unloading, travel times etc.

I also, had the customer say, if I guarantee, to be there at 3 am, he will greet me every time, he had freight with a coffee.

No matter what, I was there 99%, of the time. I rarely failed, except when line haul broke down, my vehicle broke down, to cover that, I made sure I communicated, as soon as I knew, with the customer.

At times he would, come to me or meet me at the depot to get his items.

So, as you see research and development, is the key, to sales. Make sure, you know all you can, look at all the facts, do scenarios, of what can and cannot work.

There is always, a solution to something, find it, be aware of it, don't ever promise, what you cannot deliver.

Always explain fully, to a customer and always get a confirmation, they are following what you say. By asking the right questions, the more you satisfy them, the more rapport, you build with them.

Do not ever guess or assume, to a customer in the hopes it works. Always get the facts, be confident to the customer, back what you say.

Other information, you can get from research, is a good idea with competitors' similar items. They could be the same, product, pricing, reliability, sometimes you get good, customer feedback from the internet.

Why is this a good thing to know? Well, its simple, you will then have, more knowledge, also it gives you a greater tool when dealing with customers.

Knowledge is the key; most buyers will explore all options, some will not. If you can advise a customer, in more detail, by the things you know, it will help you, to get that sale, at the end of the day, it's what all salespersons are doing.

Chapter 9

Honesty

Over the years, different industries have earned a reputation, as not being upfront. They are only about how to obtain that sale.

As I said earlier, regarding some companies, also salespersons, it's all about the sale. They don't care; if they upset a customer, there is always another.

No longer, is this an easy option, with the internet, customers can avoid your business, without you knowing. Just because, of what, another customers experience is, also the fact it's now, once it gets published for the world to see.

Customers do not always, believe what's online; some will choose, to avoid business, to save them time, based on online reviews. A lot of customers look, for a salesperson, who is honest, polite, also that will guide them, to the right purchase.

I cannot tell you, how many times, I have seen other salespersons lie to get a sale. To them, it is whatever it takes to get that sale. For an honest salesperson, like myself, I cannot and will not lie, to get a sale, simply because I know, when it happens to me, I hate it.

The biggest target, of dishonesty, is the elderly, generally because there, is a misconception they have money. So, it's easier to obtain, money from the elderly.

Sad to say, I have also seen, that too many times. I have asked, elderly customers, do they have children? Who could speak with me, as well so they understand it all too.

That way, they can discuss the purchase together and know they are making, the right decision.

Being upfront, also honest in this way, not only has gotten, my sales. It also got referrals, not just with older persons, but of course the age group of the children, for being respectful and helpful, and of course honest.

Now, of course, you don't do this, in every industry of sales, where something is not a huge investment, like a kettle. When it comes to vehicles, home improvements, that is where you, need to involve the children.

Insurance, finance or investment businesses, should have this as a mainstream measure. They are after ways to obtain, that money, for the interest of their business.

They are not exactly, lying at times, more stretching the maximum amount, of the truth.

Population always ages, new ways to scam people are tried and tested all the time. I may, not work in every industry, in my life, but I like to research.

This way when a family or friend, requires something, generally most will ring me for advice.

Not only am I researching, to protect them, but I will also guide them, where to buy based, on my research.

Sometimes, I will go as far as helping, them until completion, of the sale, either on the phone, in store, face to face or by any means necessary.

When a buyer or salesperson, is armed with the truth, so much can happen. Sales can complete with ease. You often can receive, many more leads and return buyers, with that, comes income.

My general response, to people, when asked, if I am stretching the truth just for a sale? My answer is "no." I like to sleep at night, if I run into them in the street, I want them to say hello, not swear and curse at me.

You will find that some people, do not like the truth, but those same people, do not like finding out the truth, afterward and feeling like they have been conned.

A great example is a car. There have always been the whispers, that used car yard salespersons, are the greatest, at conning buyers.

They are not, the only ones, private sellers do it also, with social media, also internet sites, allowing easier access, for anyone to sell.

It is growing fast, with con sales. Whenever I have sold, a car, like a good honest salesperson, I describe everything, that I have done to the car, what it may need, or be safe, on the road. I will also price, the car according to this.

Generally, most buyers will take the vehicle, simply because, I have been honest right from the start. I also back, what I have said.

I am sure you are saying, you cannot predict or say everything; and your right. You can be honest, say that you are unsure, if anything else may exist or be needed.

The one thing about being honest is you can always re-count, what you have said previously.

Liars generally must spin more yarn, to avoid the confrontation or deny accountability. These are the stereotypes, often referred to in our industry.

Chapter 10

We Sell Ourselves

The hardest sales job is selling ourselves; we can either undersell or oversell ourselves. Now, this is generally, when applying for jobs, once we get that job, we are then selling ourselves, to the customers, to get that sale.

As mentioned, in other chapters, buyers buy us first, if they are comfortable, with you, they buy the products or service.

Employers do the same, in an interview, the person who gets the job, is not always the most qualified. Often, it's because they, sell themselves, so well, the employer cannot let them work elsewhere.

Now, if you go an undersell yourself, often it's done because you doubt yourself. It may cost you jobs; often you feel like, if you sell yourself to well, can you keep up, to what you promised. If you fail, that will bring you down again, on how you, look at you.

Remember in the Cool Runnings movie, when they stand in front of the mirror; he says, "tell me what you see Junior." Then he says, "I will tell you what I see."

Then there are, those you cannot, find balance on how to sell themselves. Can be too confident but not cocky.

They are honest, not liars; they achieve what they state time after time.

How does one do this? It's simple; they always stay true themselves. I would rather not work, for a boss, who expects too much from me. I don't want to work, for a boss, who does not think enough of me.

We will all have days, in our lives, where we second guess ourselves, this is ok. Often, we question our life, our beliefs, our choices, then try to change ourselves.

The one thing, about sales, is, generally in most places, within the industry, it can be good for us. Everyone at times, loves to talk about themselves, in times of conversation, a customer may tell you about them, the troubles they have had, or are dealing with.

We can feel, like a counselor. We will often realize, why we are there, one to serve and assist. Two, we can often change, a person's day for 5 minutes, or their complete day, simply by listening, getting them to smile, or to make them happy.

Sales can also be our mask; we can hide behind that smile. We portray we are always, joyful. We can change the way, we do our jobs, or perform at them.

There is nothing wrong, with being upset at work, even though employers, say you won't sell anything like that. Learn to smile; you will be alright, now get out there.

Sometimes, when you get a customer, you can use the fact, you're not well today, to get a sale.

Now you are thinking, yeah right, a buyer will buy of a grumpy person. Well, not always, sometimes they feel for you, so they buy on empathy, in the hopes it brightens your day, for the next customer.

Selling ourselves, if working in a showroom or office setting, will often spark workmates, to step up and sets different moods. When you are feeling down, a little healthy banter sparks fun at work. That little competition creates a great atmosphere; customers will feel that vibe.

Chapter 11

Rewards

Ever notice, in some industries, there are rewards for performance or sales. Why is that?

Often when people, have been rewarded, be it, rewarded their performance, often they work harder. In companies, where there are, no rewards salespersons, become stagnant.

Seriously, why perform if the only reward, you get is a pay packet. The most common reward is a bonus, if you hit the projected sales, you get a bonus in your pay, or the bosses take you out for lunch, the list goes on.

Even the simplest reward, like a free office lunch once a month, or BBQ breakfast, it all works for staff on all levels. When I worked at warehouses, I have seen staff comment, their lack of enthusiasm, for the company, because previously, once a month, they had breakfast or lunch supplied, by management. In recent times, a new manager has not carried on the tradition.

It creates, a lack of support and willingness to work. When the staff thinks, why I should bother? In some factories, the back of the house, who receive and dispatch all they sell see, is the front of the house, well looked after, as they will be provided with a morning tea or lunch.

Look it does not matter, how small the reward is, the important thing is, rewards keep staff happy. It gives them purpose, to be there. Will also make them feel wanted and appreciated.

The whole concept, behind a reward, is motivation. When staff gets motivated, staff will often exceed expectations, also stay longer with your business.

Rewarding customers and clients can have a great impact, on repeat business, leading to increased sales.

Everybody wants something extra, these days, it does not, have to be expensive.

When staff are made to feel valued, as well as respected, often they will stay for longer periods. They will maintain performance, the old saying of, "dangling a carrot in front of a donkey."

Never make the reward unachievable doing this creates the opposite effect and performance will decrease, and this is not something you want.

It was once said to me, "to understand your staff expectations, you need to be able to achieve what you outline." You need to show the targets are achievable by your work and never expect someone to do what you cannot do.

Reward levels are another good practice, set them like a set of stairs as your staff reaches each step the reward increases to match performance.

Simple little rewards can have great effects try mixing it up, so it is never the same thing. Something that gets people laughing and interacting can be just as good as one expensive reward.

Another bonus which gets staff offside is the CEO bonus or hierarchy bonus. When you see a business dismisses staff due to the downturn, or rising costs and at the next financial status the CEO or hierarchy are rewarded with huge bonuses due to the profit.

Why should a CEO who is not the owner benefit any more than the staff on the ground? Now let's say if you have 2 million to pay a CEO bonus on top of what they already earn could you not split that amongst all the staff or use it to keep staff employed instead of dismissing them.

Without the staff, you don't always have a business but imagine if all staff where rewarded how much more your business could make with staff who are willing to give all they have because you look after them.

Play around with rewards and bonus structures till you get the best result and the most effective for your business.

Chapter 12

Real Estate

This is an industry that has various sections when it comes to sales but falls under two main residential and commercial.

Now when you first enter this industry, it can be daunting as; generally, it is a commissioned based income. Many first-time salespersons think that they will walk in and be on a great income often it can take 1-2 years for you to achieve high levels of income.

Of course, some are naturally born salespersons who can sell anything, but they still don't get that income any sooner as they are often still on the same percentage anyway.

Although you work in an office with other salespersons and everything on the surface seems great, often underneath other salespersons are cautious and are evaluating your every step.

See to them if you sell one of their properties they lose out on the full commission. So, they try to steer you away from their properties gently so that they can sell them first.

We are under a contract with the sellers to sell and perform our best and obtain the best price when it comes down to it. Some salespersons will often overvalue a house to obtain the client and then spend weeks or months bringing down their expectations as buyers give feedback, and eventually, you get the sale price for the market.

Now many salespersons are about converting buyers quickly but understand this is a great big investment and for first-time buyers a large step in their future.

Salespersons often make calls on customers quick after dealing with so many people they develop a list of questions to qualify how determined and ready the buyers are.

Now you're often told to qualify them as soon as possible as not to waste time and effort as this draws away from the fact you work for the seller, not the buyer.

Now to me this wrong on many levels, buyers need to be educated, and salespersons need to educate them. I was often told I spent way too long assisting buyers, but I had a reason for doing it.

The first reason is that buyer-built rapport with me, and in most cases, it stopped them buying through other agencies and agents.

Second, it allowed me to evaluate what they wanted to buy, how much they had to spend and how soon they may buy.

I remember one client I had they had been looking for two years to buy a house and dealt with many agents and agencies and they had been brushed off buy salespersons who rated them as time wasters.

Chapter 12   Real Estate

Now as I took them through home after home and talked in length when we had time amongst my schedule, I was able to picture the exact style of home they would buy. Three months I had them as my client, and one day a new property was going to be on the market, I went to the agent and said this house would be under contract first thing tomorrow.

The agent laughed and said yeh right, I smiled and said I have buyers to show first thing and this is 98% what they are after. So, my clients were the first to see the property on the first day of the market straight away as they explored you could see they had finally found it but could see some minor changes.

Within an hour of being in the home, we were filling out the contract for the full advertised sales amount. I took it back done what was needed to send it to the agent and walked into his office and said check your emails you have a contract offer full price.

He was like are you serious and I said of course I am and by afternoon the seller accepted, and it was under contract, and the wholesale went its natural course and finalized.

Now the point of this story is three agents from my office had ditched this couple and marked them as time wasters, my service to them was the best they had received, and they bought with me.

I have had other buyers do it for the exact reason I took the time to deal with them, and nothing was too hard, many times at our weekly meetings when we learned of new listings I often yelled out to the agents and said I would have a contract for you today or the next day depending on how soon I could get my clients to inspect.

By knowing my buyers, I was in a way buying for them; now this also provides a service the sellers want, a quick and easy sale.

To me being honest with buyers and sellers is the only way for me to sell, now this can be a disadvantage because although in real estate you are not to lie and mislead sellers and buyers some agents will say what you want to hear to get the contract to sell or to sell the house.

They are not essentially lying they may not mention some things or stretch other things to get the result.

I cannot do this I have my integrity and beliefs, and I know that if it happens to me, I am more than dissatisfied and only too happy to say so.

In today's world with the internet and social media sites it so easy to get caught out, lose your reputation, why would you place yourself in this situation.

The internet and social media can also boost your profile and gain you a bigger following than at times; you can handle.

Another problem within this industry is the market; some say when it is a seller market or a buyers' market configured on trends over a period or interest rates and growth.

Now there are two valuations within the market, the agent's valuation often worked out based on what them as the agent can expect to obtain from buyers in the area at the time, this is all worked out based on recent sales and trends.

Second is the bank valuation; now the bank needs to know if you default as the buyer what they can get quickly to recover the loan.

Now, of course, it easy for sellers and agents to get carried away when changes occur like industry increases population, and this creates a housing shortage, now for developers this is great they can buy large blocks of land and build. Investors get increased rent, agents get great sales figures but what happens after the quick growth slows.

Investors struggle to obtain tenants, housing prices often drop way below what investors or homeowners bought their property, this lowers their valuation then they are stuck paying mortgages they can no longer sustain and a high increase in unemployment.

Businesses close due to downturns now this has happened so many times around towns that rely on mining or exports to be healthy.

Now agents can make some great money in these booms and busts, but once it busts their income dwindles along with their reputations. Now in major cities house prices grow at such a rate it forces the average person out of the market.

Of course, homeowners want to gain profit from their investment, but they never want to lose their hard work as well.

As agents, we in some way control the market in both residential and industrial. So often I have seen after a bust in a small community the industrial sector gets greedy and it has a downward effect on the community too.

They increase the rent to cover their costs and it forces business to close then all of sudden they are earning no income, now I am not saying you cannot cover your expenses but is it not better to cover your actual outgoing and make a small profit and keep a tenant over increasing for a higher return and losing a tenant, this will also leave you without tenants longer because no business can afford your rent.

Now real estate plays its part too, they increase commissions and charges to cover the downturn in business, this is how they control markets and in the same circumstances can ruin them.

If you love talking with different people most of the time this is a great industry to work in, as no day is ever the same.

Chapter 13

Transport & Logistics

To me was an industry I always thoroughly enjoyed, and I came to be in it by pure accident. One day I was asked by a then in-law who worked in the industry if I wanted a week's work as a courier to cover a sick driver.

Now back in these days, many companies sold the runs as franchise positions, so it was your own little business and up to you sell to your customers within your area. Some companies did have salespersons for major contracts as well.

The great thing about this industry is we are all aware that without trucks Australia stops and it is the same for many countries. Why is transport such an inaugural part of our society? Well, that is because it links the raw manufacture with the manufacturer, the wholesaler to the seller and of course the end receiver you the customer.

To be good this in this industry you must be good at organizing every section extremely well although of course transport companies hire people to ensure that each section runs to exact par.

You as the salesperson need not only to know what and how your company operates and how you can slot in a new customer to deliver the service they require but to also know your competition extremely well.

Now of course even the big companies at times contract sections out or use on forwarders, and you need to know how they operate to deliver a service to your customer no good promising a service if you can not deliver.

I was lucky that not only could I network a service well I had also worked right throughout the company as well to know what drivers could and could not possibly do and I a could also reform a run to cater.

Even for successful companies, things will be out of your control not only do you need to have back up plans but also be ready to work with customers to sort it fast.

Every person in a transport company is a salesperson; the drivers must sell themselves every time they are picking up or delivering, your dispatch and customer service teams must be able to think on their feet and management must have thought of every possible scenario before it has happened.

The biggest part of transport is consistency, to be a good carrier you are under pressure all the time. It is also the biggest targeted industry for compliance.

You deal with all sections of industry, primary producers, manufacturers, wholesalers, retail & eventually the customer.

Not one client you carry for cares who else you carry for; their only concern is what you can do for them. The better the service and price the more turnover they can get from more customers.

It is a sales business that runs 24/7 365 days a year and entails so many components that can change all the time without warning. Usually well-established transport companies have already dealt with so many issues, they will have ways of dealing with the problem in place.

Chapter 14

Social Media Advertising

Since the development of the internet, as each year goes on, so do the ways to market a business. You can see that many businesses no longer need a shop front the internet is their shop front.

So, how do businessess with a storefront compete with these online businesses? It is not an easy task you can see every day on Facebook, for example, people don't even get out of their home to search for products or services they let Facebook do the work for them.

It is so easy now to post an advert on Facebook and ask for recommendations you will get all sort of reviews and recommendations based on what other people have used or know.

As a business owner these days you need to be confident in using these social media platforms or hire a person to do exactly that for you.

Before internet, businesses used phone books, tv, radio, newspaper or mailing catalogs.

Now within 1-2 minutes, a business can run a targeted ad campaign on Facebook which not only can result in more customers but also followers of your business.

Some people use social media influencers to enhance traffic to their business; this is often a cheap alternative may cost you a meal or item and sometimes costs you nothing. These social media influencers often run blogs about everything they do and where they go, but if you happen to give them bad service, everyone who follows them will know in a heartbeat.

Running your ads on Facebook can be a more direct and cheaper form of advertising with often great results but learning how to do those ads right is based on trial and error.

The internet is big business its direct service to the public in your area all the time. It is also an easier way for your competitor to know what you are offering as well. So, doing it smartly is something you must make sure you do.

Now if you still used the other forms of advertising, some ads run year to year unless you run ads in papers weekly at a huge cost or catalogs, but these are a dying service as this can be found on the internet now.

Apps are another new method now apps can serve all types of purposes, and you need to develop them to suit your customers and your business.

Let's look at Dominos Pizza once upon a time you had to ring now they have an app, from the comfort of your chair you can open it order what you wish and customize to your liking and checkout and pay no more needing cash when it arrives at your door.

Now, of course, this may not suit every business it can be hard to make an app to cater for your business, but in this changing world of finger ready buyers, you must look at every possible idea and format.

Chapter 15

Multi-Level Marketing (MLM)

MLM is big business these days and often suits those who want part-time work from home. Almost everything can be MLM these days from cosmetics, home décor, candles, pampering items, advertising, diets and the list goes on.

Why are these a big business? Well it often means lower overheads by not having shop fronts, you're not employing staff directly, it suits an array of people to undertake these kinds of positions and often the rewards or benefits are high if worked properly.

The initial setup cost may be low to medium in comparison to a franchise; you choose when you work and how you work. Often people call them a pyramid scheme, but it is far from true.

You may get into one of these businesses at any time and get rewarded by the effort you put in; this means you can also pass people who have been in longer or are above you initially.

With the internet, there is no end to finding customers you can spend an hour or eight hours the choice is yours and based on what you chose you can see your effort by the returns or bonuses you achieve. It may not be everyone's cup of tea but think about it you can work from home, you don't have to wake up rush around get ready and drive to work.

In most of these companies now you don't even have to deliver stock and most have online platforms for your customers to buy then it's delivered directly to their doors for you.

These MLM systems have made the average person be able to earn a decent income they never thought possible or even increase their current earnings which then improved their lifestyle.

Now if you were to open a small retail business outlet, yes you can build and create a website and online portal for customers to buy and you can ship too. But you're also taking on overheads like rent, power, internet, staff.

Now compare that to being at home instead of having two sets of bills you still have your rent or mortgage, power, internet you already have this in place, then these MLM companies have taken care of the website, the portal as well as logistics, so all you must do is earn and market.

Chapter 16

Get out there and sell

Not every industry will suit you, but the industry that's right for you may stem from a passion, hobby, interest or something you tried because it was different.

You may not know straight away if you want a career in one industry, sometimes you may try a few till one suits and you excel at it.

You need never to lose focus when you first start and do not expect to be rolling in 6 figure incomes right of the bat.

As you learn and grow through different industries you will adapt and develop the skills; I often find the more challenging an industry is, the better I perform.

You will only know what suits you when it happens. Do not take a job in sales because you need a job, take a job in sales where you like the challenge or are passionate about it.

Now I have not covered every single detail regarding how to sell in this book, but what I have hopefully given was some good insight.

If this book is received well, I plan to look at doing sales seminars where a more in-depth discussion will happen.

I do hope that if you have experience or even do not that something in here triggers a change or idea and wish you the most success in your future.

Notes:

Notes:

Notes:

www.ingramcontent.com/pod-product-compliance
Lightning Source LLC
Chambersburg PA
CBHW070100020526
44112CB00034B/2103